#45
Mark Twain Branch Library
9621 S. Figueroa Street
Los Angeles, CA 90003

Great White Sharks in Action

Buffy Silverman

Lerner Publications • Minneapolis

Lerner Publications Company
A division of Lerner Publishing Group, Inc.
241 First Avenue North
Minneapolis, MN 55401 USA

For reading levels and more information, look up this title at www.lernerbooks.com.

Library of Congress Cataloging-in-Publication Data

Names: Silverman, Buffy, author.
Title: Great white sharks in action / Buffy Silverman.
Description: Minneapolis : Lerner Publications, 2017. | Series: Lightning bolt books. Shark world | Includes bibliographical references and index. | Audience: Ages 6 to 9. | Audience: Grades K to 3.
Identifiers: LCCN 2016038380 (print) | LCCN 2016053869 (ebook) | ISBN 9781512433777 (lb : alk. paper) | ISBN 9781512450613 (eb pdf)
Subjects: LCSH: White shark—Juvenile literature.
Classification: LCC QL638.95.L3 S55 2017 (print) | LCC QL638.95.L3 (ebook) | DDC 597.3/3—dc23
LC record available at https://lccn.loc.gov/2016038380

Manufactured in the United States of America
1-42013-23883-11/1/2016

Table of Contents

Meet the Great White Shark

A great white shark swims in shallow water. Its dark back blends into the rocky ocean floor. Its white belly is hidden from view.

The shark's tail pushes it through the water. It steers with its fins. It speeds after a large fish.

This great white shark is as long as a giraffe is tall.

Great white sharks are the world's largest known hunting fish. Some grow to be more than 20 feet (6 meters) long!

Great white sharks live in oceans around the world. They usually swim in cool waters near the shore. But sometimes they travel far from shore.

One great white shark swam from South Africa to Australia in ninety-nine days. That's 6,897 miles (11,100 kilometers)!

Great White Grows Up

Great white sharks do not lay eggs as many fish do. Babies grow in eggs inside their mother. They grow for one year.

The babies are called pups. They hatch inside their mother. The pups eat eggs and other baby sharks!

This great white shark will soon give birth to pups.

A mother gives birth to between two and twelve great white shark pups at a time. The pups are about the size of a two-year-old child.

Great white shark pups swim away from their mom. They care for themselves.

Pups hunt stingrays and other fish.

Great white sharks often live for thirty years or more.

Great white sharks grow slowly. Males grow until they are ten years old. Females stop growing when they are fifteen. Then they are ready to have pups of their own.

Built to Swim

Look at this great white shark's narrow snout and long body. It is shaped like a torpedo! Its shape lets it zip through the water.

Great white sharks swim about six times faster than the best human swimmers.

A great white shark can swim after prey at 35 miles (56 km) per hour. Prey is an animal that the shark eats.

You breathe hard when you run. Sharks also need oxygen to move fast. Sharks take water with oxygen in it into their mouths. Gills take oxygen from the water. The water leaves the shark's body through gill slits.

Do you see gill slits on the side of this shark's head?

Parts of your nose are made of cartilage. A shark's skeleton bends like your nose.

Great white sharks do not have bones. Their skeletons are made of cartilage. They use less energy to swim fast because cartilage weighs less than bone.

Built to Hunt

Great white sharks use their strong senses to hunt. Two nostrils under the snout sniff out prey.

When attacking prey, a great white shark rolls its eyes back to protect them.

A shark's large eyes find prey in deep, dark water. It can see colors in shallow water where there is more light.

A great white's small ear holes are above and behind its eyes.

The shark's ears hear movement from prey. Pores on its snout sense electricity in the water. The electricity leads the shark to prey.

A great white shark swims under a seal. The shark rushes up. It leaps out of the water as it grabs its meal. *Chomp!*

Three hundred sharp teeth chomp the prey.

Diagram

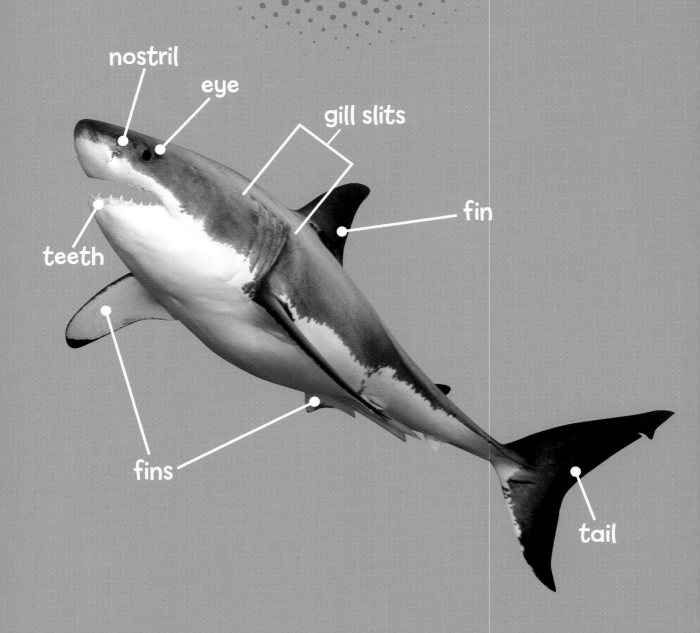

nostril

eye

gill slits

fin

teeth

fins

tail

Great White Sharks and People

- Many people fear great white sharks. But shark attacks on humans are very rare. Every year sharks bite fewer than one hundred people in the world.

- Great white sharks bite objects that they are curious about. Once in a while, they bite a person and then let go. Great white sharks don't hunt people.

- Humans are much more dangerous to great white sharks than sharks are to people. People hunt them for food and as a sport. Many people want to protect great white sharks. Some countries have passed laws to protect them.

Glossary

cartilage: bendy material that makes up a great white shark's skeleton

gill: an organ used by fish to get oxygen from water

gill slit: an opening on the side of a great white shark through which water passes

nostril: an opening on a great white shark's head through which it smells

oxygen: a gas that animals breathe

pore: a tiny opening

prey: an animal that is hunted for food

snout: the nose and mouth of an animal

torpedo: an underwater missile

Further Reading

Cleary, Brian P. *Catfish, Cod, Salmon, and Scrod: What Is a Fish?* Minneapolis: Millbrook Press, 2013.

Discovery: Great White Hot Spot
http://www.discovery.com/tv-shows/shark-week/videos/great-white-hot-spot

Discovery Kids: Great White Sharks Just Want to Nibble You
http://discoverykids.com/videos/great-white-sharks-just-want-to-nibble-you-discovery-world-safari/

Gregory, Josh. *Great White Sharks.* New York: Children's Press, 2014.

National Geographic Kids: Great White Shark
http://kids.nationalgeographic.com/animals/great-white-shark/#great-white-shark-swimming-blue.jpg

Nelson, Kristin L. *Let's Look at Sharks.* Minneapolis: Lerner Publications, 2011.

Index

Photo Acknowledgments

The images in this book are used with the permission of: © Daniela Dirscherl/Getty Images, p. 2; © Izanbar/Dreamstime.com, p. 4; © Alastair Pollock Photography/Getty Images, pp. 5, 14; © Mike Parry/Minden Pictures, pp. 6, 15, 16; © WaterFrame/Alamy, p. 7; © Pascal Kobeh/NPL/Minden Pictures, pp. 8, 9; © Yann hubert/Shutterstock.com, p. 10; © Franco Banfi/NPL/Minden Pictures, p. 11; © Stephen Frink Collection/Alamy, p. 13; © Eric Hanauer/Alamy, p. 17; © Whitepointer/Dreamstime.com, p. 18; © Peter Verhoog/Minden Pictures, p. 19; © Izanbar/Dreamstime.com, p. 20; © Wayne Lynch/All Canada Photos/Alamy, p. 22.

Front cover: © iStockphoto.com/vladoskan.

Main body text set in Billy Infant regular 28/36. Typeface provided by SparkType.